The South Beach Snacks Cookbook: On the Go South Beach Snacks Ready in Minutes

Summary

This book contains quick and easy recipes for a tastier South Beach Diet Snacking Experience. Contained are some of the quickest and easiest snacks to prepare as alternatives to some fo the high-calorie and high-sodium packaged options readily available on market today along with a number of healthy and delicious snack recipes for South Beach Diet. A guide on how to snack while in a South Beach Diet and what type of snacks to avoid are briefly outlined, too, before recipes were presented.

Table of Contents

Introduction

While South Beach Diet is, in essence, restrictive in its initial phase, nevertheless, it is not restrictive when it comes to the frequency of food intake. In fact, South Beach Diet encourages snacking twice a day—one in the mid morning and another in the mid afternoon. Experts agree that snacking leads to a more stable blood sugar. Stability in the serum levels of sugar is positively correlated with reduced food craving. Furthermore, it helps avoid being overly hungry which is one of the key components of food craving.

Snacking, however, is still governed by the rules of the diet. Not just because you are allowed to have two snacks in between meals a day, it does not mean that you could virtually gorge in to something you want. On the other hand, since South Beach Diet is caloric restrictive in nature, it does not also mean that you have to contend with blunt tasting snacks.

This book contains a list of healthier alternatives to high-calorie snacks as well as a number of delicious yet healthy recipes to help you enjoy snacking on a South Beach Diet lifestyle while still losing weight and getting an inch closer to you ideal weight.

Chapter 1: Snacking on South Beach Diet

South Beach Diet is one of the many diet programs of lifestyle that facilitate weight loss through restrictions on some foods and encouraging the consumption on others. Because the effect of South Beach Diet is determined by the initial phase (i.e. Phase I), you will be required to be particularly restrictive on food here and your diet will be composed of healthy lean protein, vegetables (with particular focus on salads), legumes, beans, cheeses, nuts, low-fat dairy and a number of god unsaturated fat sources. Phases II and III, though, needs to be given priority, too.

These stages are what constitute the later part of the diet and your initial phase to a long-term altered lifestyle. The later phases, however, are less restrictive and are easier to live with.

Though allowed to take snacks (contrary to some diet programs which are altogether highly restrictive), snacking on South Beach Diet is still governed by the rules inherent to the diet. Healthy snacks may be available for purchase in grocery stores, however, one must realize that although some may taste better, they may contain ingredients such as sugar and higher amounts of salt and may even have higher amounts of calories compared to home made ones. The best way to have access to these snacks is to prepare some for yourself and store for later.

Simple Snacking Options

Although snacks are not considered big meals since they are taken in between ones, they, nevertheless, deserves to be prepared with utmost consideration on the quality and their effects on hunger and craving. Furthermore, experts agree that dividing big meals into smaller meals taken at a shorter interval, as with snacks and small meals for breakfast, lunch and dinner bolster the metabolism—the very mechanism that determines weight gain and weight loss. A slower metabolism favors weight gain while a faster one favors weight loss.

South Beach Snacks are encouraged to be filled with vegetables and low-sugar fruits to provide for sufficient fiber which results in the feeling of fullness, delay of hunger, curbing of cravings and a healthier colon.

Although there are recipes in the succeeding chapters for healthy and delicious South Beach Snacks, here are some quick suggestions:

Raw vegetables

Although vegetables taste a lot better when cooked and seasoned, studies regarding their nutritional components establish that vitamins, minerals and some beneficial compounds are degraded when exposed to a certain temperature for a prolonged period of time or are gradually diminished.

Raw vegetables contain the most amounts of antioxidants and fiber which does not only help out with removing toxins from the colon but assist in controlling the appetite and the blood sugar level, as well.

This type of snack is best suited for South Beach Diet's Phase I which is the most restrictive of the diet phases. Among the best raw vegetable snack to munch on are celery, cucumber, cauliflower, broccoli, jicama, and bell pepper.

Kale Chips

If you used to love potato chips, you will particularly appreciate kale chips because of their texture, irresistible flavor and crunch minus the calories associated with carbohydrate based chips. Kale chips are not only good as snack but is great for parties and gatherings, too.

To make Kale chips, wash and remove leaves from step and tear them down into bite size pieces (or your preferred size) and dry them with a salad spinner. Drizzle the leaves with olive oil and add in salt for taste before baking them in an oven (previously preheated to 175 degrees celsius) for 10-15 minutes or until the edges turn brown.

You can also buy them on packaged varieties. Although they taste better, some contains large amounts of sodium which could be detrimental to a diet regimen. There are, however, low-sodium varieties which you could prefer.

Edamame

Edamame are boiled soybeans from immature pods which originated from countries as China, Indonesia, Japan, Korea and Hawaii. Normally, edamame is just prepared by boiling the soybeans and seasoning them with salt. There are, however, other versions of the recipe which adds more ingredients making the preparation tastier.

One of the variation in edamame is one which uses lemon and spices. To prepare, you will need 1 medium lemon, ½ teaspoon pepper, 16 ounces of edamame, 3 cloves of garlic and half a teaspoon sea salt.

You combine the garlic, red pepper flakes, lemon zest and 6 cups of water in a saucepan and bring them to boil (with the saucepan covered). After cooking for an additional 3 minutes after it boiled (with the cover now partially open), add in the edamame and let the water boil again before covering the saucepan for another 3 minutes. Drain and serve them in a bowl afterwards discarding the garlic and adding in salt and lemon juice for flavor.

Sunflower Seeds

If you ever feel the craving to munch at something, rather than gorge yourself in on carbohydrate-loaded snacks, why not try sunflower seeds the next time. They are equally tasty, are perfect for South Beach Diet's Phase I and are loaded with lots of nutrients as Vitamins E, B1, B2 and B3, folate, selenium, cooper, manganese, magnesium and phosphorus. In addition, sunflower seeds contain an ample amounts of omega-3 fatty acids which are known to have neuro-protective effects and are good for cardiovascular health. With these benefits, experts agree that sunflower seeds are better alternative to nuts.

There are a number of packaged sunflower brands to choose from in your favorite grocery store. Just always remember that the best ones are those with the lowest sodium contents.

Soy Nuts

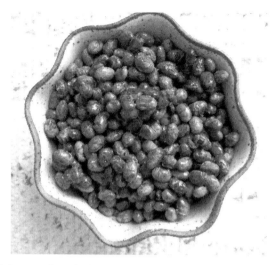

This healthy snack, which is ideal even for Phase I, is prepared in two ways: deep fried and roasted. This snack is easy to prepare, requires less ingredients, and is among the tastiest and addictive snacks for South Beach Diet.

The easiest way to make soy nuts is to soak the soy in water and baking, roasting or frying them until they are brown and crispy. Compared to peanuts, soy nuts wee found to have more protein and less fat contents. Packaged varieties offer wider options of flavor to choose from.

Carrot sticks

Take caution when eating carrots for snacks. Although they are filled with betacarotene and other nutrients, they must be taken into moderation in Phase I and is advised to be considered only on Phases II and III of the diet. Carrots, however, contain a substantial amounts of beta carotene and vitamin A in addition to its Vitamin C, Calsium and Iron contents.

The good thing about foods containing vitamin A (or beta carotene) is that, contrary to most plants, their nutritional value increases the longer they are cooked or processed.

Carrot sticks could also be consumed raw. Some people particularly like raw carrot sticks because of their sweetish flavor.

Whole-grain or whole wheat crackers

There are many crackers nowadays in various forms and flavors which serve as easy and quick snacks for many. Most crackers, however, are made of highly refined starch which spells disaster for South Beach dieters. Always remember that refined starches are very highly similar to sugar and could cause a spike in the blood sugar the same way as table sugar would. With or without metabolic-related problems, consuming foods with high sugar content could lead to lethargy after sugar high and could disrupt any existing weight-loss progress.

Whole grain, on the other hand are better because they contain lots of fiber and was prepared using complex carbohydrates or those that contains lots of minerals and nutrients in per small portion of the food. Furthermore, whole wheat (or grain crackers) contain large amounts of dietary fiber which could reduce the rate at which the body absorbs sugar and keeps the colon healthy.

Chapter 2: South Beach Diet Snack Recipes

Ham and Dill Pickle Appetizer Bites

Ingredients:

20 thinly sliced deli ham (low fat version preferred)
5 dill pickles
light cream cheese (alternatively, you can use whipped cream cheese)

Instructions:

1. Allow the cream cheese to sit at room temperature for half an hour.
2. Meanwhile, cut dill pickles in four parts lengthwise. Prepare the same number of dill pickles depending on the number of ham slices.
3. Spread a thin layer (about a teaspoon) of cream cheese to each ham slice. In doing this, remember that the ham slices need not to be covered completely in cream cheese.
4. Roll the hams with cream cheese around a slice of dill pickle. Trim the excess ham of it is longer than the pickle.

5. Place three toothpicks (of equal distance from each other) to the ham to ensure that it remains in place.
6. Cut into pieces so that each piece has one toothpick.
7. Arrange and serve on a plate. Enjoy!

Moroccan Roasted Peas

1/4 - 1/2 teaspoon Moroccan Spice Mix
1 can chickpeas (garbanzo beans; 15-ounce)
salt to taste (1/4 teaspoon kosher salt preferred)
1 ½ tbsp. olive oil (preferably extra virgin

Spice Mix:

2 teaspoon ground cumin (ground)
1/2 teaspoon sweet paprika
1/4 teaspoon ground allspice (ground)
1/8 teaspoon cayenne pepper
1/2 teaspoon chili powder
1/2 teaspoon ground cinnamon (ground)
1/4 teaspoon ground ginger (ground)
1 teaspoon coriander (ground)

Instructions:

1. Preheat oven to 177 °C. Meanwhile, drain the chickpeas using a strainer or a colander.
2. Rinse the colander using cold (or tap) water until they are no longer foamy.

3. Pat dry the beans with a paper towel or a cloth after being air-dried for 15 minutes.
4. Meanwhile, mix the ingredients for spice mix. (Tip: this mix goes well with vegetables. You could create more and store this in a jar for future use.)
5. Toss well-drained and dried beans on the olive oil, salt and spice mix.
6. Arrange them on a baking sheet in a single layer. Roast them for 40 minutes or until the beans turn slightly brown.
7. You can serve them either cool or warm.

Salsa Delight

Ingredients:

Black pepper (freshly ground)
salt
1/4 cup red onion (diced) or green onion (sliced)
1/3 - 1/2 cup Feta (crumbled)
1 diced avocado
1 cup fresh tomatoes (diced)
1 large lime, zest and juice

Instructions:

1. Juice the lime into the bowl with lime zest.
2. In a separate food bowl, dice the avocado. Add in the lime zest and juice.
3. Prepare 1 cup of diced tomatoes.
4. Meanwhile, crumble the feta and dice the onion.
5. Add in the tomatoes and red onion into the previous mix (in 2) while stirring.

6. Gently stir into the mix the crumble Feta.
7. Season with freshly ground black pepper and salt for taste.
8. Use this salsa for toasted pita chips or eat it as is.

Shrimp-Lettuce Cups

Sauce Ingredients:

2 tablespoon mayonnaisennaise
1/3 cup ketchup (use the low sugar versions or those labeled "no sugar added")
1 tablespoon lemon juice (freshly squeezed)
2-3 teaspoons cream-style horseradish

Lettuce Cup Ingredients:

1 pound shrimp
1 cup celery (sliced)
1-2 heads iceberg lettuce
1/4 cup green onion (thinly sliced)

Instructions:

1. Drain the shrimp through a colander placed in sink.
2. Whisk together the lemon juice, ketchup and mayonnaisennaise in a food bowl together with 2 teaspoon horseradish.

3. Adjust ingredients according to preference. You can add more horseradish to make your sauce spicier or you can add in more mayonnaisennaise to make it creamier.
4. Pat dry the shrimps in a paper towel after they have been drained well.
5. Cut the shrimps into pieces depending on their size.
6. Cut the lettuce in half and remove the wilted or damaged leaves on its outer surface.
7. Remove and core of the lettuce forming hollowed area where you can put the shrimp.
8. Put the shrimp mixture in the cup topped with cocktail sauce.
9. Serve and enjoy.

Turkey-Lettuce Cups

Ingredients:

1 medium-sized green bell pepper (chopped small)
salt
1-2 tablespoon green olive brine
1 can (14 oz.) crushed tomatoes
1 pound turkey (ground; fat of less than 10%)
2 teaspoon ground cumin
2-3 teaspoon Green Tabasco
2 heads iceberg lettuce
1/2 cup green olives (chopped)
4 teaspoon olive oil (preferably extra virgin)
black pepper (freshly ground)
1 can 14.5-ounce chicken broth
2 teaspoon ground coriander
1 medium sized onion (cut small)

Instructions:

1. In a large non-stick frying pan, heat 2 teaspoons of olive oil and fry the turkey over a medium heat until brown (usually 6-7 min.)

2. Push the turkey meat aside afterwards and add another 2 teaspoon olive oil.
3. Sauté green bell pepper and onion until soft and until its sides turn brown.
4. Add the tomatoes, cumin, coriander, chicken stock as well as pepper and salt according to taste.
5. Simmer for 20 minutes until the most liquid from the mixture has evaporated. Simmer the mixture over a low to medium heat.
6. Stir in Green Tabasco sauce, green olive brine and chopped green olives. Stir the mixture for 5-10 minutes to combine the ingredients well until most liquids have evaporated.
7. Meanwhile, prepare the lettuce by peeling off wilted or damaged outer leaves. Take out the core of the lettuce to form a cup and pour in the meat mixture prepared earlier.
8. Garnish each lettuce cup with slices of olive.
9. Serve and enjoy!

Barbecue Style Chicken Lettuce Cups

Ingredients

Barbecued Chicken

1/4 cup Stevia or any preferred artificial sweetener (In South Beach Diet, Stevia and Splenda are allowed)
2 teaspoon green Tabasco sauce
1/4 cup mustard (use the plain version)
2 tablespoon brown sugar
4 284-gram large chicken breasts (bones and skinless)
1 1/2 tablespoon Worcestershire sauce
1/4 cup apple cider vinegar
1/2 teaspoon Liquid Smoke
1/2 cup ketchup (Use the low-sugar version or those without sugar added. There are versions which contain artificial sweetener which is better.)
2 tablespoon tomato sauce

(You can make the lettuce wraps with Slow Cooker Pulled Pork with Low-Sugar Barbecue Sauce if you prefer.)

Lettuce Wrap

2 avocados

2-3 green onions (sliced)

1/2 teaspoon salt (or any vegetarian alternative like Vege-Sal)

1/2 teaspoon chili powder

1 tablespoons Lime juice (freshly squeezed)

2 large heads Iceberg lettuce (Tip: you can use other types of lettuces).

Instructions:

1. Remove any fatty parts in the chicken breast (i.e. chicken skin).
2. Cut the chicken breast in half (lengthwise).
3. Stir in the tomato paste, ketchup, brown sugar, apple cider vinegar, sweetener, green Tabasco sauce, mustard, Worcestershire Sauce, and the Liquid Smoke. This mix shall be your barbecue sauce.
4. Spray olive oil to the slow cooker (alternatively you can use nonstick spray) on a slow cooker.
5. Pour the sauce over until the chicken is well covered. Cook on high settings for an hour before turning back the heat to low. Cook for another 2-3 hours.
6. Cool the chicken afterwards in a cutting board until it becomes cool enough to handle.

7. Simmer the sauce in a frying pan over a medium heat for 6-8 minutes or until half of it has evaporated (or its amount reduced to half).
8. Put the chicken, afterwards, in the sauce and stir it so that the chicken becomes well coated with the sauce. Heat the chicken for few minutes of desired.
9. For the Guacamole, mix lime juice with avocado, chili powder and salt (or Vege-sal).
10. Cut out the core of lettuce to make cup and peel off the wilted or damaged outer leaves. Pour in the barbecued chicken and top it with guacamole plus sliced onions.
11. Serve and enjoy.

Shrimp-Cabbage Wraps

Ingredients:

1 small head green cabbage
1/2 cup green onion (thinly sliced)
1 pound shrimp
1 cup celery (chopped finely)

Dressing Ingredients:

3 tablespoons mayonnaisennaise
2 tablespoons light mayonnaisennaise
1 tablespoon concentrated shrimp juice

1 tablespoon lemon juice (freshly squeezed)
1 teaspoon celery seed
salt
Black pepper (freshly ground)

Instructions:

1. Thaw the shrimp overnight in the refrigerator. For shrimp juice, drain shrimp using colander and collect the drain in the bowl. Put the juice in a pan and cook over low flame to simmer until the juice is reduced to half. This juice contains the concentrated flavor of the shrimp.
2. Cut the shrimp into pieces. Slice the green onion. Chop the celery.
3. Remove the core of the cabbage using a knife. Remove the wilted and damaged outer leaves to make cups.
4. Meanwhile, whisk the mayonnaisennaise, light mayonnaisennaise, concentrated shrimp, celery seed, lemon juice, black pepper and salt. Add in the shrimp, green onion and celery into the bowl. Combine in the dressing.
5. Fill the cups with this mixture.
6. Serve immediately.

Note: This mixture can be kept for a day or two when refrigerated.

Chicken-Lettuce Tostadas

Ingredients:

Spicy Chicken:

2 tablespoon lime juice (freshly squeezed)
1 4-ounce can green chilies (diced and not drained)
4 225-g boneless chicken breast (skin removed and cut
lengthwise)
1 cup mild or medium tomato salsa
1 teaspoon onion powder
1-2 tablespoon hot sauce of your choice

Salsa:

3/4 cup fresh cilantro (chopped)
1/4 cup red onion (chopped)
1/4 cup lime juice (freshly-squeezed)
2 avocados (medium- or large-sized; diced)

For Tostadas:

8 medium-sized flour tortillas (Use low-carb or whole wheat versions)
Tomatoes (chopped)

Lettuce Wrap Tacos

2 large heads iceberg lettuce (cleaned or washed)

Instructions:

1. Remove fat and skin from the chicken breast. Cut each into half (lengthwise).
2. Spray the slow cooker with oil or non-stick spray.
3. Arrange the strips into bottom and mix in the onion powder, green chili, onion powder, tomato salsa, hot sauce and lime juice. Begin by adding one tablespoon of hot sauce and test whether you want to add in more or not depending on your level of spiciness.
4. Pour in the mixture over chicken. Cook the chicken for 5 hours or more depending on the chicken's tenderness.
5. Lay the chicken on the cutting board when the chicken is cooled down.
6. Turn the slow cooker into high settings. Leave the lid of the slow cooker partly open so the steam can come out.

7. Allow the chicken to cool and shed it into small pieces. Place the chicken into the slow cooker after being stirred into the sauce.
8. Meanwhile, peel the avocados and toss the lime juice in a large food bowl. Add in the chopped red onion and the chopped cilantro. Stir the mixture to combine them effectively.
9. Cut the lettuce into two and remove the core as well as the wilted and damaged external leaves. Fill each lettuce with a scoop of the chicken mixture and the avocado mixture prepared in 8.
10. Serve and enjoy.
11. To prepare the tostadas, preheat the oven to 300°C and toast the flour tortillas for 3-4 minutes in a toaster or oven. Spread the chicken mixture on each tortilla followed by the avocado mixture prepared in 8 (plus the chopped tomato).
12. Serve and enjoy.

Beef-Lettuce Cups

(Makes 6-7 lettuce cups)

Ingredients:

1 large head iceberg lettuce
1/2 teaspoon cumin (ground)
1/2 teaspoon garlic powder
olive oil (preferably extra virgin)
3/4 cup cherry tomatoes (chopped)
1 tablespoon Greek seasoning
¾ cup Tzatziki sauce
1 pound extra lean ground beef (use beef with as much as 7% fat)
1/2 onion (chopped finely or processed in a food processor)

Instructions:

1. Chop the onions coarsely and process them on the food processor or blender until fine. To avoid overdoing it, just pulse the processor or the blender.
2. Add in the cumin, garlic powder and the Greek seasoning before pressing the processor for few pulses until the mixture are well blended.

3. Meanwhile, put the beef and the mixture prepared in 2 in a food bowl and hand-mix the meat and the mixture to distribute the spices to the meat evenly.

4. Scoop out meat mixture and form into sphere meat balls. With the amount of mixture, you can approximately create 20 meatballs.

5. Put olive oil in a frying pan and heat it over medium heat. Cook the meatballs while occasionally turning it over to cook the meatballs on all sides for 10-12 minutes.

6. Create lettuce cups by removing cutting the lettuce in half and removing the core. Remove the wilted and damaged leaves on the outer part of the lettuce.

7. Put 2-3 meatballs on each cup. Top the cups with Tzatziki sauce and chopped tomatoes.

8. The meatballs can last for two to three days and can be used to create more cups. They can't be microwaved, though and must be heated by frying in a pan.

Beef con Sriracha Lettuce Wraps

(Makes 6-8 lettuce wraps)

Ingredients:

1-2 tablespoons Sriracha Sauce (depending on how much spiciness you can handle).
1-2 heads iceberg lettuce
1/4 cup green onion (thinly sliced)
2 teaspoon neutral-flavored oil (i.e. peanut oil or grape seed oil)
zest from one large lime
1 ½ tablespoons juice from one large lime
1 pound lean ground beef (Prefer beef with fat content of less than 10%)
1 tablespoon water
1 tablespoon fish sauce (You can use crab sauce. They taste better.)
1/2 cup cilantro (chopped)

Instructions:

1. In a heavy frying pan, heat the oil over a medium flame and sauté beef until brown and is cooked enough that the meat breaks apart.
2. Meanwhile, as you cook the meat, combine Sriracha Sauce, water and fish sauce in bowl.
3. Squeeze the juice of the lime and zest its skin. If you cannot get enough of the juice, you may use two limes).
4. Chop the cilantro and slice the green onions thinly.
5. Wash the iceberg lettuce.
6. After the beef is cooked, add in the sauce mixture prepared earlier and allow it to sizzle until all the water is lost through evaporation.
7. Stir the beef constantly to mix the flavor throughout the meat.
8. Turn the heat off and stir in the chopped cilantro, lime juice, sliced green onions and lime zest.
9. Wrap the mixture with leaves of iceberg lettuce.
10. Serve and eat with hands.

Tip: Although this is best served hot or freshly made, you can keep the mixture refrigerated to extend its life. Serve it after reheating shortly into the microwave.

Tuna-lettuce Wraps

(Makes 8 individual lettuce wraps)

Ingredients:

1 tablespoon lemon juice
2 green onions (sliced thinly)
1/4 teaspoon celery seed
1 teaspoon Dijon mustard
8 large lettuce leaves (You can use any lettuce variety such as
butter, romaine or iceberg)
1/4 teaspoon salt (or salt alternative such as Vege-sal)
1/4 cup mayonnaise or light mayonnaise
1/2 cup celery (chopped finely)
1/2 cup cherry tomatoes (chopped)
10-12 ounce canned tuna
1 tablespoon capers (chopped)

Instructions:

1. Drain the canned tuna using a strainer. Press the liquid (could either be oil or water depending on the type of canned tuna used) down the drain.
2. Meanwhile, as tuna drains, mix together the lemon juice, Dijon, mayonnaise, celery seed and salt in a food bowl. Stir the mixture well until fully mixed.
3. Cut the lettuce and separate 8 large leaves. You can use one or two heads of lettuce (depending on the size) to separate 8 large leaves and keep the inner leaves for salad later.
4. Wash the leaves thorough and let it dry or pat dry with paper towels.
5. Slice the green onions thinly and chop the capers, tomatoes and capers.
6. After the tuna has drained, stir in the dressing until they are evenly mixed before mixing in the, green onions, capers and celery.
7. Fill each lettuce leaf with the mixture prepared earlier and garnish each with chopped cherry tomatoes.
8. Serve and eat with your hands.

Tip: When in the refrigerator, this recipe can last for days to a week.

Spicy Fish-Cabbage Slaw con Avocado

(Makes 4 fish tacos)

Ingredients:

2 grilled fish (or fish fillet)
1/4 cup Greek yogurt (fat-free)
1/4 cup mayonnaise
1/4 cup buttermilk
2 tablespoon lime juice (freshly squeezed)
1 teaspoon Green Tabasco Sauce
generous pinch of ground cumin
1/4 head green cabbage (2 cups of chopped and thinly sliced cabbage)
1/8 head red cabbage (1 cup chopped and thinly sliced cabbage)
1/2 cup fresh cilantro (chopped)
1/4 cup green onion (thinly sliced)
4 large lettuce leaves (i.e. romaine, green leaf or ice berg)
1 avocado (chopped or sliced thinly)
lime wedges (for serving)
Ground cumin and lime juice

Instructions

Fish:

1. You use leftover grilled fish or you can grill one for this recipe.
2. Bring a frozen fish into room temperature.
3. Meanwhile, preheat the toaster oven or oven to 200°C.
4. Rub each fish piece with olive oil.
5. Sprinkle each with ground cumin and fresh lime juice and roast for ten to fifteen minutes until the fish turns firm when touched.

Instructions:

1. When using leftover fish, bring it out of the refrigerator and allow it to come to the room temperature.
2. Meanwhile, preheat the toaster and the oven to 200°C.
3. Place the fish (or the fillets) on a piece of aluminum foil. Sprinkle it with a tablespoon of water before wrapping and heating it in the oven for 10-15 minutes.
4. While the fish is being reheated or cooked inside the oven, whisk together in a food bowl the mayonnaise, lime juice, buttermilk, Greek yogurt, cumin and Green Tabasco. This will be the sauce or dressing mixture.
5. Chop and slice the cabbage and greed onions thinly.
6. In a medium sized food bowl, put the thinly sliced cabbage, green onions and cilantro and toss have of the dressing or sauce previously prepared. Toss an amount of sauce enough so that the cabbage slaw is well moistened.
7. Pour in the rest of the dressing or sauce into a small food bowl.
8. Remove four large outer leaves of lettuce. Prepare them by trimming the stem end and washing them. Before using, allow them to draw in salad spinner or pat dry them with paper towels.

9. Using two forks, shred the hot fish apart to reduce them into bite-sized pieces.
10. Fill each of the lettuce leaf with the fish and top them with sliced avocados and cabbage slaw.
11. Serve and enjoy

Tip: You can serve this recipe with extra sauce or dressing and lime wedges you can squeeze to add flavor. You can also keep the dressing or sauce separate with the cabbage mixture and combine them only when eating. That way, you can keep some of the lettuce for s salad later.

Oriental Pork-Lettuce Cups

(Makes about 8 lettuce cups)

Ingredients:

Dressing:

2 teaspoon ginger (pureed or you can use minced ginger)
3 tablespoon rice vinegar (prefer the non-seasoned sugar-free version)
1 teaspoon Asian sesame oil
3 tablespoon Fish Sauce (you may choose the tastier crab sauce, though)

pinch red pepper flakes

2 teaspoon garlic (pureed or you can use minced garlic)

2-3 cups shredded napa cabbage (slice less than half a cabbage thinly)

1 tablespoon canola oil (or peanut oil)

salt

8 leaves of lettuce (i.e. Iceberg, Boston or Romaine; washed and dried)

1 red bell pepper (cut into strips)

1 pound pork cutlets

black pepper (freshly ground)

Instructions:

1. Whisk together the rice vinegar, garlic puree (or minced garlic), fish sauce, ginger puree (or minced ginger), red pepper flakes and sesame oil in a small-sized food bowl. Set the dressing aside.
2. Slice the Napa cabbage thinly and cut into strips the red bell pepper.
3. Toss together the red bell pepper and the cabbage into a food bowl.
4. Meanwhile, wash the lettuce leaves and spin dry them afterwards or dry them using paper towels.
5. Make thin cutlets of pork by cutting pork chops in half. Pound the pork with a meat mallet until it is about a quarter-of-an-inch think.
6. Season the pork with freshly ground black pepper and salt on both its sides.
7. Heat a heavy frying pan over a medium flame and add oil.
8. Cook the pork for 2-3 minutes on each side or until each side turns lightly brown.
9. After the pork is cooked, cut them into thin strips and toss them with two tablespoons of the dressing mixture.
10. Afterwards, toss the red bell pepper and the Napa cabbage mixture with two tablespoons of the dressing mixture.

11. Create cabbage cups by removing the core with a life and discarding the wilted and damaged outer leaves.
12. Put 6-8 pork strips in each cup and add in a handful of the red bell pepper and Napa cabbage mixture. You can add extra dressing on top.

Tip: You can also create wraps by using lettuce leaves.

Turkey Meatball Lettuce Wraps

(Makes 9-12 lettuce wraps)

Ingredients:

Dressing:

4 tablespoons fish sauce (crab sauce makes a tastier alternative)
4 tablespoons rice vinegar (avoid the seasoned version which has added sugar in it)
2 teaspoon Asian sesame oil
½ teaspoon red pepper flakes (you can add pepper flakes later to increase the level of spiciness.

Meatballs:

2 teaspoon rice vinegar
1 tablespoons Asian sesame oil
1 tablespoons ginger root (freshly grated)
1 teaspoon garlic (minced finely)

3 teaspoons peanut grape seed oil (for frying meatballs)
1 teaspoon soy sauce (prefer low-sodium or regular version)
1 pound ground turkey (prefer turkey meats that has less than
10% fat content)

Lettuce and garnishes:

1 small cucumber, cut in thin slices, then sliced into matchstick
pieces
3/4 cup mint leaves (you can use fresh cilantro as alternative
when mint is not availab.e)
1 small cucumber (cut thinly into matchstick pieces)
8-12 lettuce leaves (romaine, ice berg or butter types are fine)

Instructions:

1. Combine the rice vinegar, fish sauce, red pepper flakes and sesame oil and allow the flavors to blend while you prepare and cook the meatballs.
2. Meanwhile grate the ginger root and chop the garlic. Combine it with rice vinegar, soy sauce and sesame oil.
3. In a food bowl, mix the seasoning mixture and the turkey using a large spoon. Since the meat mixture is relatively soft, it is advised that you chill it first for half an hour before creating meatballs. You can also make small patties (instead of meatballs) if you proceed with the soft meat mixture.
4. In a large frying pan, head 2 teaspoon of oil (grape seed or peanut oil) and make meatballs by scooping out a tablespoon-sized amount of the mixture. Add each on the hot frying pan after another.
5. In cooking the meatballs, separate them into two batches so that the cooking pan is not crowded. Cook each until they are lightly brown or are cooked through for 5-7 minutes. To cook the other batch, add another one or two teaspoons of oil.

6. Meanwhile, as the meatball cooks, wash the mint leaves and dry them with the paper towel. You can chop the cilantro if you used it instead of the mint leaves.
7. Slice the cucumber thinly. Slice them again to form matchstick-size pieces or simply chop them finely.
8. Use the inside leaves of lettuce (because they are sweet). Wash them and pat them dray with a paper towel.
9. After the meatballs are cooked, wrap 3 meatballs inside a lettuce leaf. Drizzle them with sauce and top them with the cucumber and mint (or cilantro) chopped earlier.

Oriental Spicy Turkey-Lettuce Cups

(Creates 4-6 cups)

1 tablespoons Chile Garlic Sauce (you can add more to adjust the level of spiciness)
1 1/2 pounds turkey (ground)
1 cup fresh cilantro (chopped)
4 tablespoons soy sauce
1 large lettuce head (You can use 2 small heads of butter or Boston Lettuce or a head of iceberg lettuce)
1 tablespoons peanut oil or vegetable oil (you can add more later depending on the size of you pan)
1/3 cup peanuts (chopped)
3 tablespoons red onion or shallots (minced)
1 teaspoon fish sauce
2 tablespoons ginger root (grated)
2 tablespoons garlic (minced)

Instructions:

1. Peel the ginger root and grate it using the large part of the cheese grater.
2. Chop onion and garlic and set aside.

3. Meanwhile, put a large non-stick pan over a medium flame and pour in the oil. Sauté onion for a couple of minutes before adding in the ginger root and garlic and sauté for another minute (or probably more).
4. Add more oil and put in the ground turkey. Spread out and break apart the turkey with the use of the turner. Add in the chili garlic sauce, fish sauce and the soy sauce. Cook until the turkey turns brown and crumbles apart when turned. Add the sauce and cook with a reduced flame for another five to seven minutes.
5. In the meantime, as the turkey books, wash and chop 1 cup of fresh cilantro.
6. Remove the core of the lettuce with a knife as well as the damaged and wilted outer leaves. Dry the lettuce leaves with a spinner or by pat drying it with paper towels.
7. Chop the peanuts. Put them in a small food bowl and serve them at the table.
8. After the turkey is cooked, add 1 cup of chopped fresh cilantro and cook for another 1-2 minutes.
9. Serve the lettuce cups, filling and the peanut in separate bowl. You can fill your leaf with the turkey mixture and peanut before eating.

Tip: You can also fold the lettuce over to form a taco

Turkey-Lettuce Tacos

(Makes about 8 tacos)

Ingredients:

For tacos:

1 tablespoon olive oil
1 teaspoon garlic (minced)
1-2 tablespoon green chilies (diced)
1 teaspoon cumin (ground)
1/4 teaspoon ground chipotle chili powder
1 1/2 pounds turkey (ground; it should have a fat content of less than 10%)
1/2 teaspoon salt
1/2 cup green onions (sliced thinly)
1 large bunch cilantro (finely choppedo
2 tablespoons fresh lime juice
2 large heads lettuce (You can use either romaine, iceberg, butter lettuce or Boston lettuce)

Instructions:

1. Put a heavy frying pan over a slow flame and sauté the diced green chilies and minced garlic for about a minute or until the garlic turns golden brown. Add in the ground chipotle (or cayenne) and the cumin before cooking for one more minute. Add in the turkey and salt. Break the turkey apart as it cooks and cook for about 7-8 minutes or until the turkey turned brown.
2. Slice the green onions thinly and set it aside. Meanwhile, wash the fresh cilantro and spin dry or pat dry with paper towels before chopping them finely afterwards.
3. Remove the root ends of the lettuce and the tough outer leaves. Wash the lettuce and spin them dry or pat them dry with paper towels.
4. After the turkey turned light brown, add in the green onions (sliced) and cook for another two minutes. Turn the heat off and add in 2 tablespoons of lime juice and a cup of chopped cilantro.

For salsa:
2 medium avocados
sea salt
2 tablespoons olive oil (optional)
2 tablespoons fresh lime juice
1/4 cup cilantro (chopped finely)
1 1/2 cups finely chopped cherry tomatoes

Instructions:

1. Peel the avocado and cut them into dice. Toss with lime juice in a food bowl and stir in the tomato, cilantro and olive oil.
2. Season with salt according to taste.

For the tacos:

1. Place 2 to 3 tablespoons of the mixture in a lettuce leaf.

2. Add in the meat mixture and the salsa.
3. Enjoy

Final Thoughts

You have just finished a book filled with delicious snack recipes for South Beach Diet. Experts have long since understood the importance of the role snack plays in keeping a healthy body. For one, not only does it keep the blood sugar level from dropping (or surging after taking a heavy meal), it also address hunger long before it strikes thus eliminating hunger pangs and craving. Furthermore, experts found out the dividing meals to smaller portions taken every 2 to three hours as with a South Beach Diet involving three meals and two snacks hasten the body's metabolism ensuring that the body converts calories from food (and from stored fats) into energy providing one with enough energy to conduct his day to day activities and ensuring that no excess calories are available to be stored as fats.

Snacking on South Beach Diet, particularly during the first phase, however, is difficult. For one, you are exposed to other quicker alternatives which contain high amounts of sugar and sodium—two of the factors that could undermine even other diets. In here, you were given recipes about healthy snack alternatives which you could prepare and indulge in without worrying about getting fat.

You were also presented with quick snack options—those which you do not need much preparation time—which you could opt for quick and small snack portions.

The recipes outlined here could also be used not only during your transition from phase I to phases II and III but also for years to come as you grow more into South Beach Diet.

The author hopes that you find the most out of the recipe and that you enjoyed eating them as much as preparing them.

Yours sincerely,

Stephanie

49160214R00033

Made in the USA
Lexington, KY
26 January 2016